MY
DESTINY

PRAY AND ACT ON IT

VICTORIA OLADIPUPO

MY DESTINY

Publishing Name

PVM Publishing

Publishing Website

www.pastorvictoria.org

First Edition
ISBN-13: 978-1-9161750-2-0 - E-book
ISBN-13: 978-1-9161750-3-7 – Paperback

Printed in the United Kingdom and the United States of America

Unless otherwise stated, all scripture quotes are taken from the King James Version; with emphasis added or paraphrased.

Publishing Consultants

Vike Springs Publishing Ltd.
www.vikesprings.com

For further information or contact Pastor Victoria please send an email to: pastorvictoria@ymail.com. Pastor Victoria's books are available at special discounts when purchased in bulk for promotions or as donations for educational, inspirational and training purposes.

LIMIT OF LIABILITY/
DISCLAIMER OF WARRANTY

This publication is designed to provide accurate and authoritative information in regard to the subject matter covered. It is sold with the understanding that the publisher and author are not engaged in rendering physiological, financial, legal or other licensed services. The publisher and the author make no representations or warranties with respect to the completeness of the contents of this work. If expert assistance or counselling is needed, the services of a specific professional should be sought. Neither the publisher nor the author shall be liable for damages arising here from. The fact that an organization or website is referred to in this work as a citation and/or a potential source of further information does not mean that the author or the publisher endorses the information that the organization or website may provide or recommendations it may make, nor does the cited organization endorse affiliation of any sort to this publication. Also, readers should be aware that due to the ever-changing information from the web, Internet websites and URLs listed in this work may have changed or been removed. All trademarks or names referenced in this book are the property of their respective owners, and the publisher and author are not associated with any product or vendor mentioned.

ACKNOWLEDGEMENTS

First and foremost, I would like to thank Jehovah, the Abanise that made this book a reality. Without His grace and power, I could not have written this book.

An immeasurable amount of appreciation goes to my family, the Oladipupos; and my spiritual family, Freedom House and Pastor Victoria Ministries. My deepest gratitude goes to my daughter Oluwatobi Alice for your endless help in finishing this book. You're a genius. I would also like to acknowledge the contributions of Grace, Eti, Brother Akin and Brother Segun.

To all who have contributed to the success of this book, thank you.

And to my publisher, God bless you.

FOREWORD

I pray that this book speaks to every reader in a prophetic dimension. I pray it communicates the thirst and provides the courage for all to enter into their divine destiny – that is the deep desire of my heart.

I dedicate this book to the children of God who are determined to fulfil their destiny in life, regardless of any challenges and obstacles they face.

TABLE OF CONTENTS

INTRODUCTION

God not only created you for a purpose, but He also created you with a destiny. He not only created you for a WORK, but He also created you for a GLORY. It is one thing to know WHY you are created, but it is another to understand WHAT you are created for. The WHY speaks of reasons for your existence, while the WHAT speaks about your lot, your portion, your position and your accrued benefit.

Purpose is your usefulness,
while destiny is the level of your impact.

God does not want any man to be useless to himself or herself, but He wants to beautify your life with glory, thereby enabling you to affect peoples' lives positively.

Joseph was fulfilling his purpose right from Potiphar's house, but his destiny was still far-fetched. Joseph was useful to the extent that Potiphar knew that God was blessing him because Joseph was at the helm of affairs. Joseph was a blessing to other people but not yet a blessing to himself.

Fulfilment of purpose makes you a blessing to people.
The fulfilment of destiny makes you a blessing to
yourself. Fulfilling your purpose might not change
your status, but fulfilling your destiny will change
your status for good.

"And the Lord was with Joseph, and he was a successful man; and he was in the house of his master the Egyptian. And his master saw that the Lord was with him and that the Lord made all that he did to prosper in his hand. So Joseph found favour in his sight, and he served him. Then he made him overseer of his house,

and all that he had he put under his authority. So it was, from the time that he had made him overseer in his house, and over all that he had made him overseer of his house and all that he had, that the Lord blessed the Egyptian's house for Joseph's sake; and the blessing of the Lord was on all that he had in the house and in the field."(Genesis 39 :2-5 NKJV)

Many people are so content with the testimony of what God is doing THROUGH them that they forget to ask God what He is doing FOR them.

God does not only USE people. He REWARDS them too. If He is using you to bless lives, He also wants to reward you, and He does this through the fulfilment of your destiny.

You must run life's race with two batons in hand: **the baton of purpose** and **the baton of destiny**. Many people are only running with the **baton of purpose**, downplaying the role of destiny. We believe if anyone can find his or her usefulness in life, that person will automatically make it in life, and this, of course, explains why many destinies go unfulfilled. As we continue in the pursuit of purpose, we must also check that we are following the template He gave us in order not to fall short in any way.

Destiny and purpose are the two wings needed to fly like an eagle in life.

When one, especially destiny, is not known or present, one cannot get to the highest altitude God planned for them.

This book in your hand is to correct this anomaly and to open us up to all we need to know and do to fulfil destiny in grand style.

My prayer for you is that this book will unravel the flood of revelation in it to you. Also, my prayer is that God will not leave you at the verge of purpose, but that He would also bring you into the fulfilment of destiny in Jesus' name. Amen!

Happy reading.

CHAPTER 1

UNDERSTANDING DESTINY

This chapter explains in detail what destiny is all about. DESTINY is a word that is virtually absent in Christianity today. I truly believe that every born-again Christian should be interested in their destiny and how to fulfil it before the second coming of our Lord Jesus Christ, as that is the reason for your existence. As mentioned in Luke 19:13, whatever has been given to us as Christians, we must use it to maximise our destiny and fulfil God's mandate by doing business till He comes.

Many people are now interested in purpose, but they do nothing to understand the powerful connection of both destiny and purpose.

ACCORDING TO DICTIONARY.COM

Pur·pose is defined as

1. the reason for which something exists or is done, made, used, etc.

2. an intended or desired result; end; aim; goal.

Des ti ny—noun

1. something that is to happen or has happened to a particular person or thing; lot or fortune.

2. the predetermined, usually inevitable or irresistible, course of events.

A TV has a purpose but no destiny. Gas and electricity both have a purpose but no destiny. The bills you have to pay are given with a purpose but no destiny. However, all living things that the Lord places His breath of life into have both purpose and destiny. That is the difference between something that is merely purposed and someone who is born and destined to be what they need to be. Even unbelievers have a divinely given purpose and destiny.

This is destiny:

"Moreover, whom He predestined, these He also called; whom He called, these He also justified; and whom He justified, these He also glorified." (Romans 8:30 NKJV)

"For the earnest expectation of the creature waiteth for the manifestation of the sons of God". (Romans 8:19 KJV)

We can examine the life of Joseph as a case study. He is one of the Bible personalities who reveals the power and effect of purpose and destiny in a man's life. Joseph was one of the twelve sons of Jacob, the son of Isaac. Joseph and Benjamin were born of Rebecca, who Jacob loved. Joseph, as a young man, was despised by his brothers because of the love that his father had for him.

His destiny is revealed in Genesis 37:5-7 and 9.

"Now Joseph had a dream, and he told it to his brothers; and they hated him even more. So he said to them, 'Please hear this dream which I have dreamed: There we were, binding sheaves in the field. Then behold, my sheaf arose and also stood upright; and indeed your sheaves stood all around and bowed down to my sheaf.'" (Genesis 37:5-7 NKJV)

"Then he dreamed still another dream and told it to his brothers, and said, 'Look, I have dreamed another dream. And this time, the sun, the moon, and the eleven stars bowed down to me.'" (Genesis 37: 9 NKJV)

His vision: Genesis 50:20

"But as for you, ye thought evil against me; but God meant it unto good, to bring to pass, as it is this day, to save much people alive. Psalm 105:17-21

"He sent a man before them, even Joseph, who was sold for a servant: [18] whose feet they hurt with fetters: he was laid in iron: [19] until the time that his word came: the word of the Lord tried him. [20] The king sent and loosed him; even the ruler of the people and let him go free. [21] He made him lord of his house, and ruler of all his substance."

God's purpose for his life, which was the reason for action, was revealed in Genesis 49:8–12.

"Judah, you are he whom your brothers shall praise; your hand shall be on the neck of your enemies; your father's children shall bow down before you. Judah is a lion's whelp; from the prey, my son, you have gone up. He bows down, he lies down as a lion; and as a lion, who shall rouse him? The sceptre shall not depart from Judah, nor a lawgiver from between his feet, Until Shiloh comes; and to Him shall be the obedience of the people. Binding his donkey to the vine, and his donkey's colt to the choice vine, He washed his garments in wine, and his clothes in the blood of grapes. His eyes are darker than wine, and his teeth whiter than milk." (Genesis 49:8-12 NKJV)

Destiny is the destination. Purpose is the pathway that takes you there.

Purpose is an inevitable route to destiny.

Jesus, in purpose, came to save us from sin through His death, but He was destined to be our Lord and Saviour, and He eventually had to submit to His purpose, in order to fulfil His destiny!

Destiny is God's goodwill towards us as individuals, while purpose is the work we must put in as individuals to allow God's goodwill to come to pass (Jeremiah 29:11).

Destiny and purpose are twain together, and I believe that they are both essential for the fulfilment of what we are created for.

"And we know that all things work together for good to those who love God, to those who are the called according to His purpose." (Romans 8:28 NKJV)

God has a wonderful destiny and purpose for you in His kingdom.

No matter what mistakes you have made
in the past, I want you to know that
God has not given up on you.

He still loves you and is cultivating you and developing you into the man or woman of character that He has called you to be (John 3:16, Romans 5:8, Jer. 31:3). He will make you a pillar of strength in His house where you shall impact others mightily for His glory.

*The function of time fulfils destiny, and the
devil targets it by delaying its fulfilment.
The enemy does not attack you because of your past;
he troubles you because of your future — your future is
his primary target (John 10:10)!*

In as much as we know that delay is not denial, delay can be very dangerous - especially when it is satanic. John 10:10 states the thief comes to steal, kill and destroy.

"Then he said to me, *'Do not fear, Daniel, for from the first day that you set your heart to understand, and to humble yourself before your God, your words were heard; and I have come because of your words. But the prince of the kingdom of Persia withstood me twenty-one days; and behold, Michael, one of the chief princes, came to help me, for I had been left alone there with the kings of Persia.'"* (Daniel 10:12-13 NKJV)

*The enemy can delay destiny, but with
perseverance, it can be fulfilled.*

Today, I decree and prophesy that despite delay, you will fulfil your destiny in Jesus' name. Amen!

David is another example of a godly man whose destiny appears to have come forth "later than necessary" if viewed from a human perspective. You know the story: Samuel anointed him king, and God's favour brought him into the king's court. Then David had to flee for his life, pursued by his enemy – King Saul.

WHAT IS DESTINY THEN?

The Bible is the authoritative handbook of destiny. Destiny dates back to the time before the birth of a child (Jer. 1:5).

- Destiny is what God has created you to be, even while in your mother's womb.

- Before you were created, destiny was God's original plan.

- Destiny is God's placement for your life.

- Destiny is the splendour or glory of your assignment on earth (Genesis 45:13).

- God had a picture of your destiny in His mind before He created you.

- Your habitual decisions determine your destiny.

- If it is divine, the Holy Spirit will supervise its fulfilment.

- Your destiny may be dependent on the fulfilment of other peoples' destinies just as many destinies are waiting for the fulfilment of your destiny (II Chronicles 16:9 NKJV).

Jeremiah 1:5 (NKJV):

"Before I formed you in the womb I knew you; before you were born I sanctified you; I ordained you a prophet to the nations."

---

*Before you were born, God already knew
who you were to be.*

God created you specially to become a solution to the world.

---

*Before God gave you life, He already
chose you for greatness.*

You were not born by mistake but by the divine will of God.

You might be useless in the eyes of men,
but you are useful in the sight of God.

You might be nobody in the eyes of men,
but you are somebody in the eyes of God.

Men might have rejected you,
but God has accepted you.

Do you know why God created you? Do you know what your destiny is?

Think about this as we journey into how to discover your destiny.

CHAPTER 2

HOW TO DISCOVER YOUR DESTINY

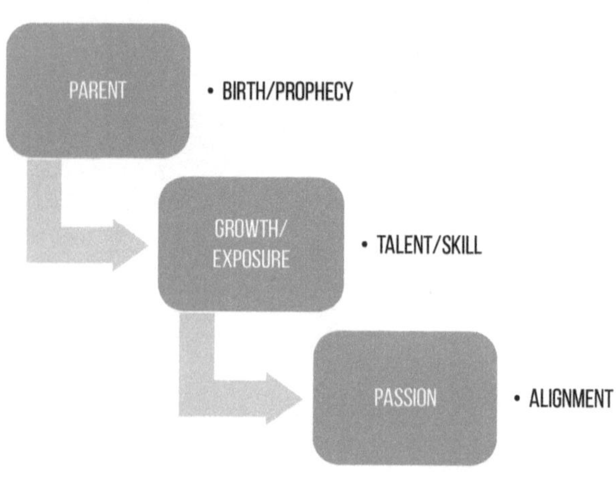

The God we serve is a God of purpose. Everything He created from the unseen to the seen exists and comes into being for a purpose. From the smallest particles of matter to the largest mammals, to the majestic mountains and oceans, to the countless stars in the universe, all of these display God's majesty, might and wisdom (Genesis 1). There is purpose for every design. Have you observed that most of the fruits rich in vitamin C (sour fruits like oranges, limes, etc.) are harvested during the rainy season? Have you ever wondered the purpose for the seasons (winter, summer, etc.) (Genesis 8:22)? If you could take time to be curious and ask the purposes of the things around you, you will be amazed that all things have a purpose for existence.

You are not on earth to create destiny,
but you are here to fulfil it.

How do you fulfil what you do not know exists?

"Before I formed you in the womb, I knew you; before you were born, I sanctified you; I ordained you a prophet to the nations." (Jeremiah 1:5 NKJV)

"Each of us, as a good manager of God's different gifts, must use for the good of others the special gift we have received from God." (I Peter 4:10 TEV)

The first thing to note is that destiny exists, and it has been predetermined before you were born. Who predetermined it? God. We must go to the person who predetermined it.

The above scripture fully confirms that you have a predetermined destiny, and fulfilling that purpose must be your primary mission in life. You have been gifted with a special gift!

Furthermore, for you to fulfil your assignment, you must first know what it is. If we say your assignment on earth is your purpose, then you must discover it before it can be fulfilled.

Your fulfilment, satisfaction and peace of mind are all tied to that purpose and destiny!

"How do I find my God-given destiny?" I get asked this question consistently. Many people have no clue why they were born. In this book, you will learn how to discover your God-given purpose and fulfil destiny.

To discover your God-given purpose, you must go to the person who gave it (Genesis 1:27 and Genesis 2:7).

"Call unto me, and I will answer thee, and show thee great and mighty things which thou knowest not." (Jeremiah 33:3 KJV)

God gave each of us an operator's manual when He created us. It is called the Bible - the written Word of God. It is sharper than a double-edged sword. It penetrates even to dividing soul and spirit, joint and morrows, and it judges the thoughts and attitudes of the heart (Hebrews 4:12).

Our operator's manual also tells us which counsellor to inquire of concerning this critical issue.

Isaiah 9:6

"For unto us a child is born, unto us a son is given: and the government shall be upon his shoulder: and his name shall be called Wonderful, Counsellor, The mighty God, The everlasting Father, and The Prince of Peace."

Our counsellor is none other than the Lord God Almighty!

He is not just any counsellor. Read Isaiah 9:6 again! He is our Wonderful Counsellor! He is the only one who can reveal to us our God-given purpose.

When you seek His counsel, there is no possibility of you failing in life because His counsel is excellent in working (Isaiah 28:29).

*Your destiny is unique and freely given
but needs to be discovered.*

I Cor. 2:9-12 (KJV)

"But as it is written, Eye hath not seen, nor ear heard, neither have entered into the heart of man, the things which God hath prepared for them that love him. But God hath revealed them unto us by his Spirit: for the Spirit searcheth all things, yea, the deep things of God. For what man knoweth the things of a man, save the spirit of man which is in him? even so the things of God knoweth no man, but the Spirit of God. Now we have received, not the spirit of the world, but the Spirit which is of God; that we might know the things that are freely given to us of God."

So, the Holy Spirit is the revealer of secrets. Jesus said His father would send the Comforter in His Name, who will teach you all things and reveal it to us. Whatever He tells us is TRUE because He is called the SPIRIT OF TRUTH (John 14:26).

'For God speaketh once, yea twice, yet man perceiveth it not. In a dream, in a vision of the night, when deep sleep falleth upon men, in slumberings upon the bed. Then he openeth the ears of men, andsealeth their instruction. That he may withdraw man from his purpose, and hide pride from man. He keepeth back his soul from the pit, and his life from perishing by the sword." (Job 33:14-18 KJV)

Joseph didn't find his destiny in the field or while playing or watching TV. God revealed it to him in a vision or dream. Dreams are one major way God reveals destiny to people.

"And Joseph dreamed a dream, and he told it his brethren: and they hated him yet the more. And he said unto them, Hear, I pray you, this dream which I have dreamed: For, behold, we were binding sheaves in the field, and, lo, my sheaf arose, and also stood upright; and, behold, your sheaves stood round about, and made obeisance to my sheaf." (Genesis 37:5-7 KJV)

Habakkuk sought out the Wonderful Counsellor, and He became a man of understanding and got a clearer view of his God-given vision.

Habakkuk 2:1-3

1 I will stand upon my watch, and set me upon the tower, and will watch to see what he will say unto me, and what I shall answer when I am reproved.

2 And the LORD answered me, and said, Write the vision, and make it plain upon tables, that he may run that readeth it.

3 For the vision is yet for an appointed time, but at the end it shall speak, and not lie: though it tarry, wait for it; because it will surely come, it will not tarry.

Note the sequence of events...

1. You must engage in earnest prayer (Habakkuk 1:1-17).

2. Next, get quiet before the Lord (Habakkuk 2:1).

3. The Wonderful Counsellor will speak to you (Habakkuk 2:2).

4. When He speaks, write it down (Habakkuk 2:2).

5. Be ready to convey your God-given vision to others (Habakkuk 2:2).

6. Rejoice, because God's vision for your life is coming to pass (Habakkuk 2:3).

You must ask God what your destiny is. What has He created you for? What has He bestowed in you? I have some great news for you! The Lord we serve hears and answers us. When you ask, answers will be given (Matthew 7:7).

He will answer you, but how you hear Him depends on your level of spiritual growth and development (Hebrews 5:13-14).

Those who pay attention to the words of God maintain a pure heart through forgiveness and repentance, and those that obey what He communicates with them will hear from Him easily (Mark 4:20).

Those who do not give heed to His word or take time to soak in presence, practise unforgiveness and do not repent of their sins will struggle with hearing the voice of God (Mark 4:14-19).

You need to get to a place of quietness, a secret place, and spend some time in the presence of God (Isaiah 30:15).

It might require a change of vocation, location, behaviour, attitude or beliefs.

It might require you to re-train yourself, and it might require you to humble yourself or start afresh.

Note that the plan of God for your destiny is easily found in the Word of God, so you have to jumpstart your study of God's word.

Genesis 1:27-28 *"So God created man in His own image, in the image of God created He him; male and female created He them. And God blessed them, and God said unto them, Be fruitful, and multiply, and replenish the earth, and subdue it: and HAVE DOMINION over the fish of the sea, and over the fowl of the air, and over every living thing that moveth upon the earth."* (KJV)

Jeremiah 29:11 *"For I know the thoughts that I think toward you, saith the Lord, thoughts of peace, and not of evil, to give you an EXPECTED END."* (KJV)

John 15:16 NKJV - *"You did not choose Me, but I chose you and appointed you that you should go and bear fruit, and that your fruit should remain, that whatever you ask the Father in My name He may give you."*

Ephesians 2:10 KJV

"For we are his workmanship, CREATED IN Christ Jesus unto good works, which God hath BEFORE ORDAINED that we should walk in them."

There is a working that is ongoing in you, and this is to make sure you fulfil destiny. This work is dated back to eternity before you were born. He knew you, called you by a name, ordained and sanctified you for this special thing called DESTINY.

This working entails packaging you with gifts and opportunities to showcase that which is on your inside. God cannot load you with gifts and not create the platform for the gift to be used. These gifts are meant to drive you into destiny as you work on your purpose in life.

Romans 8:29-30

"For whom He did foreknow, He also did predestinate to be conformed to the image of His Son that He might be the firstborn among MANY brethren. Moreover, whom He did predestinate, them He also called: and whom He called, them He also justified: and whom He justified, them He also GLORIFIED."

The end of every destiny is GLORY. Every destiny undergoes these workings as pointed out in the scripture above, and they are informed of states:

- State of foreknowledge
- State of predestination
- State of conforming to the image
- State of being called
- State of justification
- State of glorification

You need to analyse and take inventory of your gifts, talents and abilities. Your purpose is inextricably linked with your gifts and talents.

The major link between destiny and purpose is that if you get your purpose wrong, you will be fulfilling another man's destiny.

Getting your purpose right has placed you on the path to fulfil destiny, and this is the reason you need to take inventory of your gifts, talents and abilities even after praying to God to reveal them to you.

Before your birth, God deposited in you all of the necessary gifts, talents and abilities you would need to fulfil His purpose for your life.

In your quiet time, in the secret place, ask God how you can serve Him and others. Understand that you have a vital part to play in this world.

You are a hero, a person of extreme significance. You have a mandate and a mission here on planet Earth. A large aspect will be in service to others. Challenge yourself to do this daily and ask God how.

Are you seeking your purpose in life? Many of us do not ask this question until we receive a wake-up call in the form of a crisis. We then wonder what the meaning of our lives really is.

We are to seek a deeper meaning for our lives.

Everyone is born with a higher purpose in life, and to discover it takes some inner searching.

Here are some ways to help you find your purpose in life:

1. What do you love to do that brings you joy? Look at your hobbies and your work. What do you do that

you become so engrossed in because it is exciting and absorbing?

2. What are you good at doing? Your family and friends can tell you what your talents and skills are. Write down what you are good at.

Do you like being with people or have an affinity with children or creating beautiful things? Are you task-oriented, do you love to write, communicate or teach?

3. Meditate. Deep within you, you have the answers you are seeking, and to find them, your mind needs to be clear.

Discovering your purpose in life can take as little as ten minutes a day if you sit still and ask. Have patience and keep asking until you receive the answer, and then follow through by taking the first step towards it, and then you will be shown the next step.

4. Look to your past. As a child, what were you always doing that perhaps you were scolded for at home or school? I remember receiving a report from my needlework teacher, which said, "Victoria should work more and talk less."

At the time, the teacher thought that my talent for communicating and listening to others was a hindrance in her classroom. Now, I am using that same talent in my work. What did you do as a child? The answer to this question is your natural ability that you are to use in your purpose.

5. What comes naturally to you that you enjoy doing and would do even if you were not paid for it? Do you find that people trust you with their problems, or do you find yourself frequently teaching others how to do things? You may find that you are a nurturing person who nurses others, or maybe you find yourself conveying interesting facts to others when you socialise.

---

*Your purpose in life will bring you joy and
contribute to other peoples' lives in some way.
If you feel that your life is meaningless right now,
it is time to sit still and uncover what you are
really here to do.*

Focus on what you love to do. What is that one thing in your life that you absolutely love to do more than anything? That thing that gives you inexplicable passion and zest for life? Think about it. What is that thing for you? It doesn't matter what it is — it only matters that you love to do it more than anything, that when you do it, you feel alive like you've never felt before. Spend time thinking about this, and make sure that you find that special thing in your life.

Joseph used his gifts in Potiphar's house and in prison before he finally came into destiny. Learn to serve with your gifts. How faithful you are with your gifts in the place of service may hasten the delivery of your destiny into your hand.

The last key is perhaps a little easier, but it still requires thought! You need to continually check in with your feelings to see if you're on the right track. As you did in the first step, get quiet and go within — meditate. Think about what you're doing and how you feel about it. Does it make you feel great? Does it make you excited to get up in the morning, like you can't wait to greet the coming day to see what's in store? If you're not feeling this kind of passion about what you're doing, you need to re-think what's actually most important to you.

Your divine purpose is within you.

You don't need to go out into the world to find what it is. You will need to do that to follow that purpose, but to find it, all you need to do is ask yourself what you love to do and how you can serve others with that talent. Give it a shot. Use your mind and ask yourself for the answers. Your mind will give them to you! And by your mind, I mean a renewed mind that has been fine-tuned by the word of God (Romans 12:2).

"For everyone that useth milk is unskilful in the word of righteousness: for he is a babe. But strong meat belongeth to them that are of full age, even those who by reason of use have their senses exercised to discern both good and evil."(Hebrews 5:13-14 KJV)

CHAPTER 3

THE PLACE OF PEOPLE IN DESTINY

*God has a purpose and plan for this world,
and man is an important part of it.*

The existence of the universe and everything in it is according to the purpose of God. Man is essential in the scheme of executing God's purpose and plan. The purpose of God for man is that man should be His ambassador on earth (II Cor. 5:20). God has different assignments for each person for which He endows specific skills, talents and benefits (Rom. 12:6; I Cor. 12:4).

*Purpose stresses your value in the lives of people,
while destiny underscores the usefulness of people
in your life.*

The scripture says woe to him that is left alone. A man who is without anyone in life is a failed destiny waiting to happen (Ecclesiastes 4:10).

"And Adam gave names to all cattle, and to the fowl of the air, and to every beast of the field; but for Adam there was not an help meet for him." (Genesis 2:20 KJV)

Adam was already fulfilling purpose by naming the animals but yet to fulfil destiny because he was alone. God saw that he needed a companion to fulfil what He has assigned him to do on earth.

*Nobody fulfils destiny in isolation.
You need the gift of men to fulfil the prophecy
hanging over your life even as you pursue purpose.*

"Now these were the men who came to David at Ziklag while he was still a fugitive from Saul the son of Kish; and they were

among the mighty men, helpers in the war, armed with bows, using both the right hand and the left in hurling stones and shooting arrows with the bow. They were of Benjamin, Saul's brethren." (I Chronicles 12:1-2 NKJV)

"And they helped David against the bands of raiders, for they were all mighty men of valor, and they were captains in the army. For at that time they came to David day by day to help him, until it was a great army, like the army of God." (I Chronicles 12:21-22 NKJV)

Men made David great. **These men came with different abilities to help him succeed.**

The fulfilment of destiny is at the mercy of the quality of people you have around you.

You need men to turn the kingdom to you. You need men to establish your kingdom. The fulfilment of destiny is never a one-person show.

Lone rangers don't go far in destiny. You need the company of the right people to succeed in life.

"For by wise counsel thou shall make a war: and in the multitude of counsellors there is safety." (Proverbs 24:6 KJV)

"Without counsel purposes are disappointed: but in the multitude of counsellors they are established." (Proverbs 15:22 KJV)

"Where no counsel is, the people fall: but in the multitude of counsellors there is safety." (Proverbs 11:14 KJV)

When you don't have people, purposes are disappointed, and destinies are frustrated.

Hear the wisdom of the preacher on this subject in Ecclesiastes 4:8-12:

"There is one alone, and there is not a second; yea, he hath neither child nor brother, yet is there is no end of all his labour, neither is his eye satisfied with riches; neither saith he, for whom do I labour, and bereave my soul of good? This is also vanity, yea, it is a sore travail. Two are better than one; because they have a good reward for their labour. For if they fall, the one will lift up his fellow: but woe to him that is alone when he falleth; for he hath no another to help him up. Again, if two lie together, then they have heat: but how can one be warm alone? And if one prevails against him, two shall withstand him; and a threefold cord is not quickly broken."

When you do not have people, the struggle continues. The Bible says there is no end to your labour. May that not be your portion in Jesus' name. When you have people, the Bible says there is a good reward for your labour.

"In the multitude of people is the king's honour: but in the want of people is the destruction of the prince." (Proverbs 14:28)

The sittings of the servants and the attendance of the ministers in Solomon's kingdom were two major things Queen Sheba saw, and there was no more strength in her (I Kings 10:1-7, emphasis: verse 5).

People that are meant to affect your life positively and give expression to your gifting are called **destiny helpers**. The major destiny helper you need is the Holy Spirit. He is the one that will connect you to the destiny helpers in human form.

The Holy Spirit is your helper. The Holy Spirit's purpose and desire is not to hinder you but to help you (John 14:26).

John 14:16-18:*"And I will pray the Father, and He will give you another Helper, that He may abide with you forever, even the Spirit of truth, whom the world cannot receive, because it neither sees Him nor knows Him; but you know Him, for He dwells with you and will be in you. I will not leave you orphans; I will come to you."* (NKJV)

John 16:7: *"Nevertheless I tell you the truth. It is to your advantage that I go away; for if I do not go away, the Helper will not come to you; but if I depart, I will send Him to you."* (NKJV)

John 15:26: *"But when the Helper comes, whom I shall send to you from the Father, the Spirit of truth who proceeds from the Father, He will testify of me."* (NKJV)

WHO IS THE HOLY SPIRIT?

The Holy Spirit is the third Person of the Trinity of God. The Spirit is a person and deserves respect, honour and gratitude.

HOW DOES HE HELP YOU?

The Spirit is not constrained to a single method of help. Here are some of the ways He wants to help you – if you give room for Him to do so:

- **In Prayer**

  Romans 8:26 NKJV: *"Likewise the Spirit also helps in our weaknesses. For we do not know what we should pray for as we ought, but the Spirit Himself makes intercession for us with groaning which cannot be uttered."*

The Spirit knows all things. He will help us to pray accurately and effectively.

One way the Holy Spirit does this is by giving us tongues to pray in the language of the angels in direct communication with God. Although we may not understand what we are saying, we know that, as our prayer is Spirit-led, it is under the will of God.

II Corinthians 14:2: *"For he who speaks in a tongue does not speak to men but to God, for no one understands him; however, in the spirit he speaks mysteries."*

Jude 1:20:*"But you, beloved, building yourselves up on your most holy faith, praying in the Holy Spirit."*

- **He guides us**

The Spirit gives precise directions. He can help with what we say, who we marry, our finances and even our journey routes.

Romans 8:14: *"For as many as are led by the Spirit of God, these are sons of God."*

Acts 16:6-7: *"Now when they had gone through Phrygia and the region of Galatia, they were forbidden by the Holy Spirit to preach the word in Asia. After they had come to Mysia, they tried to go into Bithynia, but the Spirit did not permit them."*

John 16:13 NKJV: *"However, when He, the Spirit of truth, has come, He will guide you."*

- **He teaches us all things**

John 14:26a NKJV: *"But the Helper, the Holy Spirit, whom the Father will send in my name, He will teach you all things."*

- **He reminds us of the Word**

John 14:26b NKJV: *"But the Helper, the Holy Spirit, He will bring to your remembrance all things that I said to you."*

- **He tells us things to come**

John 16:13 NKJV: *"However, when He, the Spirit of truth, has come, He will tell you things to come."*

- **He declares to us the things of Jesus**

John 16:12-15 NKJV: *"I still have many things to say to you, but you cannot bear them now. However, when He, the Spirit of truth, has come, He will guide you into all truth; for He will not speak on His own authority, but whatever He hears He will speak; and He will tell you things to come. He will glorify me, for He will take of what is mine and declare it to you. All things that the Father has are mine. Therefore, I said that He will take of mine and declare it to you."*

• He abides with us

John 14:16-18 NKJV: *"And I will pray the Father, and He will give you another Helper, that He may abide with you forever, even the Spirit of truth, whom the world cannot receive, because it neither sees Him nor knows Him; but you know Him, for He dwells with you and will be in you. I will not leave you orphans; I will come to you."*

The Holy Spirit is God's gift to us. It is God Himself living in us, and He will never leave us.

Should we give room for the Spirit to lead us, He will.

• He empowers us to be witnesses

Acts 1:8 NKJV: *"But you shall receive power when the Holy Spirit has come upon you; and you shall be witnesses to Me in Jerusalem, and in all Judea and Samaria, and to the end of the earth."*

• He brings life and healing to us

Romans 8:11 NKJV: *"But if the Spirit of Him who raised Jesus from the dead dwells in you, He who raised Christ from the dead will also give life to your mortal bodies through His Spirit who dwells in you."*

• He encourages us

Romans 8:16 NJKV: *"The Spirit Himself bears witness with our spirit that we are children of God."*

II Corinthians 13:14 NKJV: *"The grace of the Lord Jesus Christ, and the love of God, and the communion of the Holy Spirit be with you all. Amen."*

Destiny helpers in human form have divine ties.

Some people are in your life for a season,
and some for a reason, but destiny helpers
are for life!

"Then Jonathan and David made a covenant, because he loved him as his own soul." (I Sam 18:3 NKJV)

Destiny helpers are people God has pre-positioned
on your way, even before your vision or assignment
was made known to you.

They have words of encouragement to keep you going. They will be there for you when you need to make crucial decisions. They will always be there for you. They are ready to go to any lengths to see you succeed. Many times, they are angels from God who take the form of humans working for you.

Examples abound in the Bible. Saul had a servant with him when he was looking for his father's lost donkeys (I Samuel 9:5-6). Naaman had such a servant with him when he went to seek a solution for his leprosy (II Kings 5:10-12).

Elisha was that to Elijah, just as Joshua was to Moses.

I pray the Lord will grant us the grace to recognise that these helpers are from Him when we meet them.

Relationships are a beautiful thing,
and some are ordained by God.

God says it is not good for man to be alone. All relationships ordained by God are designed to empower us and help us become the people God created us to be. There is a place we may never get to in life until somebody comes into our lives – destiny helpers.

Relationships are relevant in a man's life, and we need to cherish them and do all we can to maintain those that are purposeful.

Exodus 4:27 NIV: *"The LORD said to Aaron, "Go into the desert to meet Moses." So he met Moses at the mountain of God and kissed him."*

God usually sends different types of destiny helpers your way, and this is evident in the life of Moses. These are the Jethros, Aarons and Joshuas.

The Jethros:

It is important to have mentors in life. You can learn a lot from people who have been where you are heading (Horeb International).

They have the experience and the scars to share with you. Their counsel comes from experience, so you do not have to go through the same struggles they did.

A mentor has something that you admire and lack, but you need to be discerning to locate the right ones.

The good ones are great teachers. Jethro, Moses' father-in-law, gave him sound advice concerning his leadership of the nation. Moses was wise enough to appreciate the advice and apply it, which improved his leadership effectiveness (Exodus 18).

We all need mentors, and Jesus was no exception.

How did he learn to preach and to proclaim social justice?How did Jesus learn about vital rituals like baptism? It was from one who became famous for going around "proclaiming a baptism of repentance for the forgiveness of sins." It was from one who baptised Jesus himself.

Throughout scripture, mentoring is something that is seen very regularly to help people grow in their relationship with God. One could call it a one-on-one discipleship method (Jake Kircher). It is God linking you with another to learn from them and be a partner in what they are doing. Examples are Elijah and Elisha, David and Jonathan, Naomi and Ruth.

Mentoring was also evident between Jesus and his disciple John, who is referred to five times as "the disciple whom Jesus loved". Likewise, with Eli and Samuel in the Old Testament, and multiple times with Paul, first being mentored by Barnabas and then mentoring Titus.

The question to think about also is if mentoring is so important to success in sports, business and other areas of life, and if mentoring, or one-on-one discipleship, was modelled and supported in scripture, why do we so rarely see mentoring today when it comes to our own relationships with God?

Jesus himself modelled mentorship. Jesus called them one by one and discipled (mentored) them to go out and do the same.

Hence, what is mentoring?

Mentoring is when someone who has "been there, done that" takes someone who is "getting there, doing that" under their wings.

Let me repeat that. Mentoring is when someone who has "been there, done that" takes someone who is "getting there, doing that" under their wings. I define mentoring this way for two reasons:

First, mentoring isn't as much about age as it is about experience. As Barnabas mentored Paul, the two men very well could have been similar in age, but Barnabas had the experience with a relationship with God that Paul didn't have.

Secondly, often when we think about being a mentor, people are swift to discredit themselves because they haven't "lived a good enough life". In reality, though,

it is often the people who have made the most mistakes that have the most to offer in a mentoring relationship.

Again, Paul is a great example of this seeing that before he became a Christian, he killed Christians for a living. If Paul had the grace to mentor, anyone can. Another example is Elisha and Elijah.

I Kings 19:19-21:

"So he set out from there, and found Elisha son of Shaphat, who was plowing. There were twelve yoke of oxen ahead of him, and he was with the twelfth. Elijah passed by him and threw his mantle over him. He left the oxen, ran after Elijah, and said, 'Let me kiss my father and my mother, and then I will follow you.' Then Elijah said to him, 'Go back again; for what have I done to you?' He returned from following him, took the yoke of oxen, and slaughtered them; using the equipment from the oxen, he boiled their flesh, and gave it to the people, and they ate. Then he set out and followed Elijah and became his servant."

I think this is the hardest part. Things that stop people from having or starting a relationship are funny. People are intimidated, embarrassed or proud and don't want help. If you think or act as if you know more than me but you want me to mentor you, it would be challenging.

You need to spend time together, work with your mentor and be trained by him. Who is training you? Mentoring is one-on-one discipleship.

---

*Fulfilling your destiny is to learn it
and be trained for it.*

I am not your mentor if we don't have one-on-one conversations. I am not really mentoring you if we never sit together and have a conversation. However, in case your mentor is far from you, you must endeavour to get all their materials, whether they be books, audiotapes or other kinds. This gives you access to their wisdom. You should still make attempts to develop a formal contact with them in which they know he or she has a protégée in you via mail or telephone calls.

Paul said to the Philippians, "Brethren, join in following my example", (3:17) and "The things you have learned and received and heard and seen in me, practice these things." (4:9)

If you're not walking with me, you will not see me do those things.

And thirdly, which should be the result of the first two steps, is love and respect one another deeply. When you get close to some people, they start to disrespect you.

It is no hidden fact how much Paul deeply loved Timothy by the way he speaks about him in his letters to the Philippians. In Paul's letters, he calls Timothy a son four times. Paul, just like a real father, so earnestly cared about him and encouraged him. Paul also expressed tough love with him as well. Paul encourages him, gives him some advice and corrects Timothy in his thinking.

The good mentor's teaching is not his own ideas. Jesus told the crowd, "My teaching is not my own."

---

*A good mentor's teaching is based on
the Word of God.*

Jesus further said his teaching comes from the One who sent Him. In other words, His teaching is inspired by God and given by God.

Jesus, as fully human, habitually waited upon God in prayer, and God revealed His thoughts concerning man to Him to convey to man. Jesus' teachings were solidly the direct words of God.

In the same vein, a good mentor is someone who waits on God in prayer; he is a prayerful person who studies the Bible frequently and practices what the Bible says.

If you seek to do God's will, you will know the right mentor. Jesus also stressed that "if anyone chooses to do God's will, he will find out whether My teaching comes from God or whether I speak on my own." That is, if you are someone who is seeking to do what is right by God, you have the zeal to know God's will concerning your life, and you desire to follow His will, then you will intuitively know whether someone who comes into your life is a good mentor or a bad mentor. *If you are thirsty for water and someone gives you Sprite in a glass pretending it is water, you will know as soon as you take a sip of the drink.* In the same way, if you strive seriously to do God's will and you are looking for solid godly mentoring, you will know it when you get it.

To guard against bad mentors masquerading as wolves in sheep clothing, I urge you to seek to know Christ and do God's will.

"Do not conform any longer to the pattern of this world but be transformed by the renewing of your mind. Then you will be able to test and approve what God's will is-- his good, pleasing and perfect will." (Romans 12:2 NKJV)

"Fix your thoughts on Jesus, the apostle and high priest whom we confess." (Hebrews 3:1 NKJV)

"Fix your eyes on Jesus, the author and perfecter of our faith." (Hebrews 12:2 NKJV)

"Love the LORD your God with all your heart and with all your soul and with all your strength." (Deuteronomy 6:5 NKJV)

Seek first the kingdom of God and its righteousness (Matthew 6:33). Surrender yourself completely to God, and God will send you the right mentor.

The Aarons: These are your prayer partners. They pray with you until something happens. They are part of your generation and demand the best for and out of you. This category of people is your closest friends.

"As iron sharpens iron, so a man sharpens the countenance of his friend."(Proverbs 27:17 NKJV)

"He who walks with wise men will be wise, but the companion of fools will be destroyed." (Proverbs 13:20 NKJV)

It is extremely important to decide on those we intend to keep as friends and companions, for their influence can play a very vital role in our destiny, for good or bad. Aaron wasn't solely Moses' brother, but also his best friend, aid and companion throughout his leadership years and in the wilderness. Your Aaron is your spiritual high priest, lifting you up in prayer constantly before God.

The Joshuas: Your Joshua can be referred to as your Timothy, who will lift your hand and empower you to leave a legacy behind. It would be a waste of life if all you accomplished were to come to earth to eat, drink and die without leaving a legacy behind. We have a great and energetic generation coming behind us, and it's very vital that you influence them to be higher, stronger and greater than us, just like the generation of Jethros. To leave a good legacy, it is very vital to build and train people who will exceed our accomplishments. Moses equipped and developed Joshua to be a mighty leader. Joshua was able to do what Moses could not, and that was to move the Israelites into the promised land.

DESTINY QUENCHERS

Genesis 37:1-20

We are not here by chance, and we do not live aimless lives. We are a people of destiny.

God has a purpose and a destiny for your life, but there are destiny quenchers who never want us to get to our God-appointed destination.

The destiny of Jesus was to be the Saviour of the world (John 4:42; Luke 19:10). However, the devil tried to kill Him many times – for instance, by stoning to death or pushing Him down a steep hill. (Luke 4:28-30; John 8:40, 59).

The devil did not want Jesus to die on the cross to secure salvation for man. Even a trusted disciple was manipulated to stand in His way (Matthew 16:22-23).

*Never allow yourself to be a
candidate of circumstance.*

Do not travel by the winds of chance. Discover your divine destiny and map your way to it. There is power to deal with destiny quenchers. Never let them intimidate you.

*Any vessel that God has an interest
in will have an equally vested interest
from the devil.*

In the beginning, God had a purpose for creating man, and the devil caused a breach by enticing man, so man sinned against God. "And the serpent said unto the woman, ye shall not surely die" (Genesis 3:4 NKJV).

Joseph was also a man of destiny, whom Potiphar's wife wanted to destroy, but he stood for God, and he fulfilled destiny. However, Samson was destined to be great, but his passion for women destroyed his destiny, and he died as a blind hero. Our Lord Jesus Christ came to fulfil divine purpose, but Satan entered Peter to counteract the purpose. Jesus recognised the spirit and rebuked him.

"But he turned, and said unto Peter, get thee behind me, Satan: thou art an offense unto me: for thou savourest not the things that be of God, but those that be of men."

(Matthew 16:23 KJV)

Brethren, you are destined to fulfil the purpose of God for your life, but to be able to achieve this, you need to be like the sons of Issachar.

"And of the children of Issachar, which were men that had understanding of the times, to know what Israel ought to do; the heads of them were two hundred; and all their brethren were at their commandment."

(I Chronicle 12:32 KJV)

PURPOSE AND DIVINE QUEST

Genesis 1:26-27; 37:5-11; James 3:9; Isaiah 54:14-17; Jeremiah 29:11; John 10:10; 3 John 2; II Corinthians 9:8; II Thessalonians 3:16

From the very beginning, God created man for a purpose – to be like God in everything:

"Let us make man in our image. So God created man in His own image, in the image of God created He him; male and female created He them." (Genesis 1:26,27; James 3:9)

On the surface, this statement looks ordinary but contains tremendous truth about the destiny of man. Think for a moment about this: God never suffers defeat. God can never go into captivity. **God has never lost a battle. God cannot experience affliction or oppression. God only knows freedom, liberty, dominion, success, victory and achievement. God reigns in majesty and glory. This is meant to be the believer's portion (Isaiah 54:14-17).**

Man, who was created in the image of God, was meant to live a similar kind of life, enjoying victory and success, basking in the sunshine of dominion and enjoying the rarefied air in the mountain of achievement.

God's first mandate to man, which has remained unchanged is Genesis 1:28: *"Be fruitful and multiply, and replenish the earth, and subdue it: and have dominion."*

After God created man, He blessed man (Genesis 1:28). The curse came as a later development because of disobedience (Genesis 3:16-19). However, we are living at a time when God is bringing restoration of all things to His original plan, purpose, intention and design. Do not allow yourself to be left out.

*"For I know the thoughts that I think toward you, saith the Lord, thoughts of peace, and not of evil, **to give you an expected end.**"*

(Jeremiah 29:11 KJV)

God gave Joseph two distinct dreams which portrayed God's destiny for his life (Genesis 37:5-11). The dream was given twice because it was certain to come to pass: *"And for that the dream was doubled unto Pharaoh twice; it is because the thing is **established by God**, and **God will shortly bring it to pass.**"*

(Genesis 41:32 KJV)

PLOT OF DESTINY QUENCHERS

Revelation 13:10:

"He who leads into captivity shall go into captivity; he who kills with the sword must be killed with the sword." Here are the patience and faith of the saints.

(a) Destiny quenchers always manifest great hatredtowards people of destiny. Joseph was MUCH favoured and MORE loved than his brothers. The father bought him *"a coat of many colours"*, and this angered his brothers, and *"they hated him and could not speak peaceably unto him"* (Genesis 37:3, 4).

What special favours are you enjoying? Are there glorious opportunities that are opening for you? Expect the activity of destiny quenchers.

(b) Telling destiny quenchers your dreams, aspirations, goals and purpose can only increase their hatred.

"And Joseph dreamed a dream, and he told it his brethren: and they hated him yet more" (Genesis 37: 5 KJV).

(c) When destiny quenchers see your star and God's plan for your greatness, it infuriates them.

"And his brethren said to him, shalt thou indeed reign over us? Or shall thou indeed have dominion over us? And they hated him yet the more for his dreams, and for his words" (Genesis 37:8 KJV).

Also, God's plan for Israel was great, but Balak was a destiny quencher. God had blessed Israel. Balak wanted the blessing cancelled or reversed and for a curse to replace it (Numbers 22:11-12; 23:7-11).

(d) Envy and jealousy are the trademarks of destiny quenchers.

*"And his brethren **envied** him: but his father observed the saying"* (Genesis 37:11 KJV). Envy and jealousy for your potential always saturate the system of destiny quenchers.

Furthermore, Daniel and the three Hebrew children were prospering in Babylon. The destiny quenchers hated them and plotted against them (Daniel 3:1-28; 6:1-25). However, the persecution only resulted in further greatness, promotion and favour (Daniel 3:29, 30; 6:26-28).

The activities of destiny quenchers will catapult you to greatness in Jesus' name. Amen.

(e) The substance of the plan and plot of destiny quenchers is always EVIL. *"But as for you, ye thought evil against me; but God meant it for good"* (Genesis 50:20 KJV).

The thoughts of destiny quenchers are evil,
although their words may be sugar-coated and
their actions cloaked with apparent love.

The substance of their thoughts and action are, at the very best, only poison coated with honey. The end of it is always destruction and ruin. Delilah was a destiny quencher whose words swayed Samson. Her purpose was to nullify Samson's anointing and power and to render him useless (Judges 16:4-21).

(f) Conspiracy and murder are familiar watchwords in the dictionary of destiny quenchers.

*"And when they saw him afar off, even before he came near unto them, **they conspired against him to slay him.** And they said one to another, behold, **this dreamer cometh.** Come now therefore, **and let us slay him**, and cast him into some pit, **and we shall see what become of his dreams**."* (Genesis 37:18, 20)

POWER AGAINST DESTINY QUENCHERS:

Genesis 37:18,20; 42:6; 45:3; Psalm 118:17-18; 23:6; Daniel 3:29-30; 6:26-28; Numbers 23:7-11,19-25; 24:10.

Destiny quenchers may be sinister and deadly,
manipulative and satanic, but they do not have
the final say in our destiny. We can get to our
God-appointed destination irrespective of their plot,
and we can inherit our divine destiny despite
their devilish plans.

Despite their conspiracy to kill (Genesis 37:18, 20), *"I shall not die, but live, and declare the works of the Lord"* (Psalm 118:17). God has not given you

over to death; why should you die? (Psalm 118:18).
You will not die until you fulfil your destiny in Jesus'
name. Amen.

Destiny quenchers think they will waste your life
and shatter your dreams, and in mockery, they declare
"and we shall see what will become of his dreams" (Genesis
37:20). However, in a positive, definite and divine-
engineered way, they will see what will eventually
become of your dreams. You will become Egypt's
Prime Minister like Joseph, and they will see it (Genesis
42:6; 45:3). You will receive further promotion like
Daniel and the three Hebrew children, and they will
see it (Daniel 3:29, 30; 6:26-28). You will be blessed
by Balaam contrary to Balak's expectation (Numbers
23:7-11, 19-25; 24:10). It will lead them to gnash their
teeth (Psalm 112:9-10).

Joseph's brothers' plan was meant for evil, but God
meant it for good, so also God will prepare a table
before you in the presence of your enemies: He will
anoint your head with oil and your cup will run over
(Psalm 23:5). They plan to kill you, but *"**surely** goodness
and mercy shall follow you all **the days of your life**"* (Psalm
23:6).

Some things increase your power and victory over
destiny quenchers:

(i) Righteousness (Daniel 6:22; I John 5:18; Isaiah
54:14-17). Righteousness exalts a nation. Keep yourself
from guile. Don't be caught in the trap of sin.

(ii) Goodness: Never repay evil for evil. It is natural
to want to retaliate in the same coin when you are hurt,
but we must not, as we have the nature of Christ.

CHAPTER 5

DESTINY CLINIC

Satan's daily pursuit is to render destinies useless by afflictions and termination. He often exploits man's free will to disobey God to pollute destinies.

---

*To fulfil your divine destiny in life,
you need to subject yourself to constant
thorough spiritual examination
in the destiny clinic.*

When the devil can't quench your destiny with all the evil onslaughts and attacks thrown at you, it is possible to be scared or hurt, even by people who you think should have been of help. The purpose of the destiny clinic is to treat you back to health: spiritually, psychologically and emotionally.

"And they found an Egyptian in the field, and brought him to David, and gave him bread, and he did eat; and they made him drink water; and they gave him a piece of a cake of figs, and two clusters of raisins: and when he had eaten, his spirit came again to him: for he had eaten no bread, nor drink any water, three days and three nights. And David said unto him, To whom belongeth thou? And whence art thou? And he said, I am a young man of Egypt, servant to an Amalekite; and my master left me, because three days agone, I fell sick. We made an invasion upon the south of the Cherethites, and upon the coast which belongeth to Judah, and upon the south of Caleb; and we burnt Ziklag with fire."

(I Samuel 30:11-14)

King David lost all he had worked for all his life to an invasion of the Amalekites. The invasion was so strategic that everybody in the army of David lost everything. The loss was national, and David wept till he had no strength to weep again. The destiny of David and the people with him was almost dead, but David encouraged himself in the Lord.

When men fail and every soothing word
of comfort has lost its savour,
God always makes the difference.

David was wounded, but his healing process started immediately after he encouraged himself in the Lord.

God is the great physician. He is the chief medical officer in the clinic of destiny. When you have Him, you are sure in a safe haven, even in the midst of storms. There will be no loss of lives or property. David never apportioned blame. He took the right steps and action, and his eyes of mercy were still open, even when he was still mourning himself. His mission to recover his people was not so important that he would not save a dying soul on his journey to Amalek.

*When you are hurt in the
journey of destiny, try and heal or
treat the hurting you meet on your way.*

Never say you're too busy with your own problems to help others.

*The tool for recovery of destiny is in
helping other hurting folks around you.*

Joseph got this revelation on time, and it paid well for him. He was conspired against, sold, lied about and put in prison for a wrong course, which he never committed. In all these, he never lived in unforgiveness; neither was he lonely nor moody. Rather he was cheerful, motivating other prisoners and checking on them to know how they were faring.

"And Joseph came in unto them in the morning, and looked upon them, and behold they were sad. And he asked Pharaoh's officers that were with him in the ward of his lord's house, saying, Wherefore look ye so sadly today?"

(Genesis 40:6-7 KJV)

Jabez's destiny was thwarted by his mother at birth. Jabez was never resentful towards his mother. He took the right step to pray, which enrolled him in the destiny clinic.

*Prayer is the enrolment form that gets
you admitted into the destiny clinic.*

"And Jabez was more honourable than his brethren: and his mother called him Jabez, saying because I bare him in sorrow. And Jabez called on the God of Israel, saying, oh that thou wouldest

bless me indeed, and enlarge my coast, and that thine hand might be with me, and that thou wouldest keep me from evil, that it may not grieve me. And God granted him that which he requested."

(I Chronicles 4:9-10 KJV)

When a destiny sustains an injury and is left untreated, the following can happen:

- Born great but die unknown.

- Born as a warrior but die as a slave.

- Born as a champion but operate as a loser.

- Born to adorn people with costly dresses but wear rags.

- Born a millionaire but live as a pauper.

- Born as a human goldmine but now wretched and poor.

- Born to be the head but now operate at the tail region.

- Born as a world changer but now a victim of frustration and despair.

- Born a runner but now a crawler.

- Born with eagle wings but now flapping life with chicken wings.

Why do people fail to fulfil their destiny?

1. The flesh *(Galatians 5:18-21).*

2. Evil foundations *(Exodus 17:14-17; Joshua 6:26 - fulfilled I Kings 16:34).*

3. Spiritual dryness.

4. Household wickedness.

5. Negative internal attitudes *(Philippians 4:8).*

6. Covered sin.

7. Curses.

8. Rejecting the process of God for your life.

9. Slackness in pursuing divine destiny *(Joshua 18:1-3)*.

10. Demonic cobwebs.

11. Prophetic manipulation.

12. Pride.

13. Bad health.

14. Disobedience.

15. Wrong company.

16. Wrong selection of a spouse.

17. Fear.

18. Lack of commitment.

19. Impatience.

20. Collective captivity.

Prescriptions for destiny recovery and fulfilment:

1. Pray to discover the person you are supposed to be.

2. Have genuine and complete repentance *(Acts 2:38)*.

3. Have genuine new birth.

4. Be passionate about fulfilling your destiny.

5. Confront and conquer destiny robbers, wasters, killers and polluters.

6. Seek for complete deliverance of your destiny.

7. Live an exemplary Christian life.

8. Submit yourself to the leadership of the Holy Spirit and God-ordained authority.

9. Consecrate your life to the Lord and live a life of holiness and humility.

10. Pray without ceasing to discover and recover your destiny *(John 18:37)*.

11. Live ready to forgive those who hurt you.

12. See beyond the hurt, see it as a process God ordained to train you.

PRAYER POINTS

Genesis 37:3-8, 18-20; 50:20; Nehemiah 1:12, 16-18; Judges 16:4-21; Numbers 22:11,12; 23:7-11; Daniel 3:1-28; 6:1-25.

Prayers against killers of my destiny (These prayers are taken from several blogs or sermons: Dr DK Olukoya, Emmanuel and Blessing Agbo, Anointed Child of God, Pastor Charles Godfrey and Mabrig Korie Ministries):

1. I command any power using my destiny, the destiny of my spouse or the destiny of my children to die in Jesus' name!

2. Any power, any man or woman that has hijacked my destiny, wherever you are, I command you to end up in death like Adonijah in Jesus' name!

3. Any Adonijah in my life fighting for my destiny, I command you to die in Jesus' name!

4. Satan, I remove from you the right to rob me of my divine destiny in the name of Jesus.

5. I command all powers of darkness assigned to my destiny to leave and never return in the name of Jesus.

6. I destroy every demoter assigned against my life in the name of Jesus.

7. I command all the enemies of Jesus Christ that have access to my progress to leave and never return in the name of Jesus.

8. I paralyse every satanic opportunity contending against my life in the name of Jesus.

9. Every incantation, ritual or witchcraft power against my destiny, fall down and die in the name of Jesus.

10. I render null and void the influence of destiny quenchers and swallowers in the name of Jesus.

11. Every household wickedness struggling to re-arrange my destiny to lose your hold in the name of Jesus.

12. Any eye that is watching my star to bring it down, I command to be destroyed by the arrows of fire in the mighty name of Jesus.

13. Let every satanic conspiracy against my destiny be broken by fire in the mighty name of Jesus.

14. I command every Ahitophel counsel given against my life shall be turned to foolishness in the name of Jesus.

15. I command that every satanic power ordained and mobilised to cast me down be roasted by the fire of God in the name of Jesus Christ.

16. I decree and declare that my star will surely findme, as the star of Jesus located Him.

17. I decree that the wise men sent on my behalf will surely locate me in Jesus' name.

18. I decree and declare that as the wise men locate me, they will come with precious gifts.

19. Any power released from the satanic kingdom or from any coven to pursue me, even in my dreams, I command to fall and die in Jesus' name.

20. Any grave that has been dug for mylife,I command to begin to swallow those that dug it. The Bible says he that digs a pit shall fall into it.

21. I come against every limitation in my life.I command them to be broken in Jesus' name.

22. O God, any destiny destroyer released against my life, somersault and die in Jesus' name.

23. I command every circle of frustration existing in my life to be broken in Jesus' name.

24. I will not commit suicide; neither shall the death of my destiny come at my own hand in Jesus' name.

25. Every power released to put me to shame, be roasted by the fire of God in Jesus' name.

26. I command every serpentine tongue ordained against my life to be cut into pieces in Jesus' name.

27. Every curse of 'thou shall not excel' operating in any area of my life, your time is up – breakin the name of Jesus.

28. In the presence of those saying,'we shall see what will become of his dream', o God arise and catapult me from glory to glory.

29. The enmity between my destiny helper and me be destroyed.

30. Take me from where I am to where I will fulfil my purpose.Isaiah 45:11 says, *"Thus saith the Lord, the Holy One of Israel, and his Maker, ask me of the things to come concerning my sons, and concerning the work of my hands **command ye me."***

31. Reveal to me my destiny, God.

32. I disannul all the tricks of the devil towards my destiny for it is written, greater is Jesus Christ that dwells in me than the devil that is in the world.

33. I reject to be a picture of failure.

34. I refuse to be abased, rejected, forsaken, desolate and downcast.

35. I render null and void the influence of destiny destroyers in the name of Jesus.

36. Every destiny destroyed by curse be reversed now in the name of Jesus.

37. I render every power contending with my destiny powerless in the name of Jesus.

38. I paralyse every satanic strategy contending against my ministry, family and life in the name of Jesus.

39. I bind every demon working against my destiny in Jesus' name.

40. I release the fire of God and the blood of Jesus to destroy the root of every spirit speaking against my destiny in the name Jesus.

41. I hold the blood of Jesus against every altar speaking against my divine destiny.

42. I hold the blood of Jesus against every power using the heavenlies against me.

43. I release the fire of God and the blood of Jesus and destroy every witchcraft, curse, spell, vexes, enchantment and mind control, I return them to the sender a hundredfold. I bind it to them by the blood of Jesus. Amen.